FIRST 50 WORSHIP SONGS
YOU SHOULD PLAY ON GUITAR

ISBN 978-1-70514-884-0

Visit Hal Leonard Online at
www.halleonard.com

World headquarters, contact:
Hal Leonard
7777 West Bluemound Road
Milwaukee, WI 53213
Email: info@halleonard.com

In Europe, contact:
Hal Leonard Europe Limited
1 Red Place
London, W1K 6PL
Email: info@halleonardeurope.com

In Australia, contact:
Hal Leonard Australia Pty. Ltd.
4 Lentara Court
Cheltenham, Victoria, 3192 Australia
Email: info@halleonard.com.au

Amazing Grace
(My Chains Are Gone)

Words by John Newton
Traditional American Melody
Additional Words and Music by Christ Tomlin and Louie Giglio

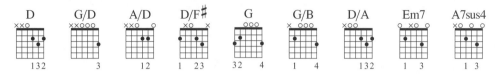

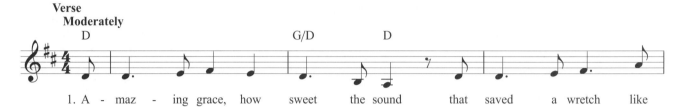

Verse
Moderately

1. A - maz - ing grace, how sweet the sound that saved a wretch like

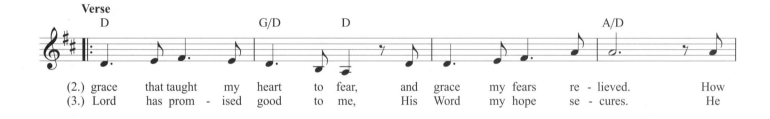

me. I once was lost but now I'm found, was blind but now _ I see. 2. T'was

Verse

(2.) grace that taught my heart to fear, and grace my fears re - lieved. How
(3.) Lord has prom - ised good to me, His Word my hope se - cures. He

pre - cious did that grace ap - pear the hour I first _ be - lieved. }
will my shield and por - tion be as long as life _ en - dures. }

My chains are

Chorus

gone, I've been set free. My God, my Sav - ior _ has ran-somed me. And like a

flood, _____ His mer - cy rains un-end - ing love, ___ a - maz - ing

grace.   3. The grace.   My chains are

grace.   4. The earth shall soon dis - solve like snow, the

sun for-bear to shine.   But God, who called _ me here be - low, will

be for - ev - er mine,   will be for - ev - er

mine.   You are for - ev - er mine.

3

Battle Belongs

Words and Music by Phil Wickham and Brian Johnson

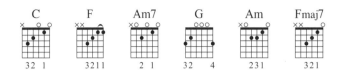

Verse
Moderately

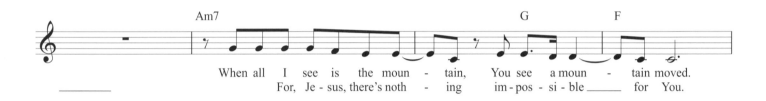

1. When all I see is the bat - tle, You see my vic - t'ry. _____
2. And if You are for _____ me, who can be a - gainst _____ me? _____ Yeah. _____

_____ When all I see is the moun - tain, You see a moun - tain moved.
For, Je - sus, there's noth - ing im - pos - si - ble _____ for You.

And as I walk through the shad - ow, Your love sur - rounds _____ me. _____
When all I see are the ash - es, You see the beau - ty. _____ Thank You

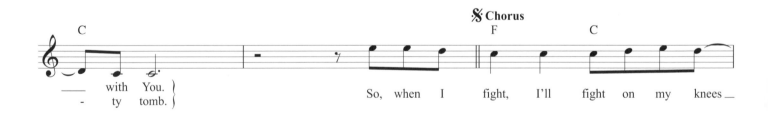

God. There's noth - ing to fear _____ now, for I am safe _____
When all I see is the cross, _____ God, You see the emp -

%Chorus

_____ with You. } So, when I fight, I'll fight on my knees _____
- ty tomb. }

_____ with my hands lift - ed high. _____ Oh God, the bat - tle be - longs to _____ You. And ev - 'ry

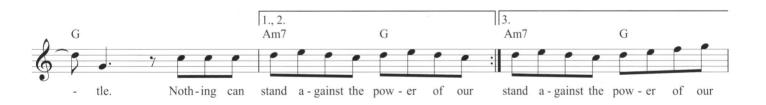

Because He Lives, Amen

Words and Music by William J. Gaither, Gloria Gaither, Daniel Carson,
Chris Tomlin, Ed Cash, Matt Maher and Jason Ingram

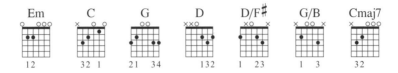

Verse

Moderately

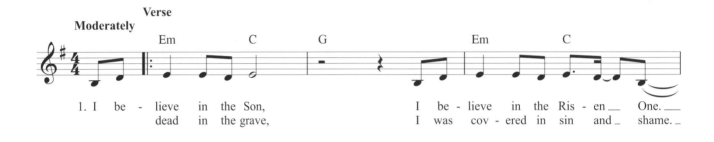

1. I be - lieve in the Son, I be - lieve in the Ris - en __ One. __
dead in the grave, I was cov - ered in sin and __ shame. __

_____ I be - lieve I o - ver - come by the pow - er of His __ blood.)
_____ I heard mer - cy call my __ name. He rolled the stone a - way.)

Chorus

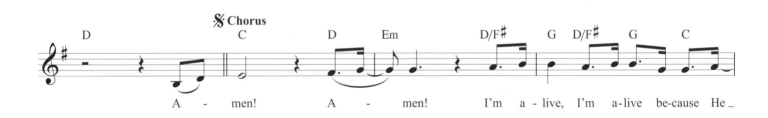

A - men! A - men! I'm a - live, I'm a-live be-cause He __

To Coda

__ lives. A - men! A - men! Let my song join the one that nev - er __

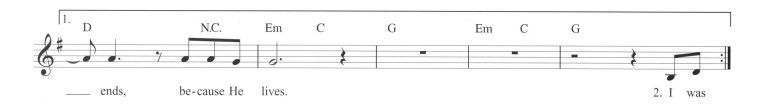

1.
_____ ends, be-cause He lives. 2. I was

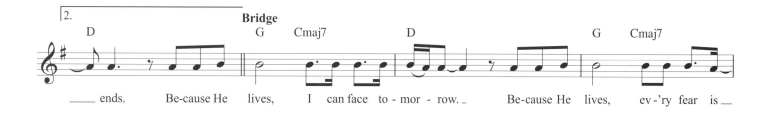

2. **Bridge**
_____ ends. Be-cause He lives, I can face to-mor-row. _ Be-cause He lives, ev-'ry fear is _

D.S. al Coda
_____ gone. I know He holds my life, my fu-ture in His _____ hands. A -

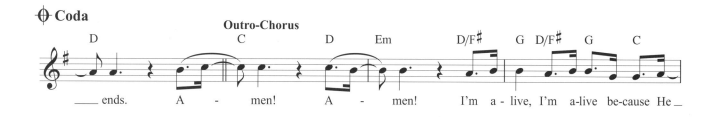

Coda
Outro-Chorus
_____ ends. A - men! A - men! I'm a - live, I'm a-live be-cause He _

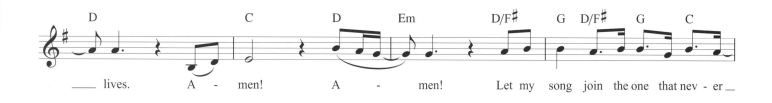

_____ lives. A - men! A - men! Let my song join the one that nev-er _

_____ ends, be-cause He lives. _____ be-cause He lives. _____

Blessed Be Your Name

Words and Music by Matt Redman and Beth Redman

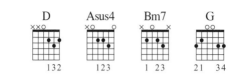

Verse
Moderately

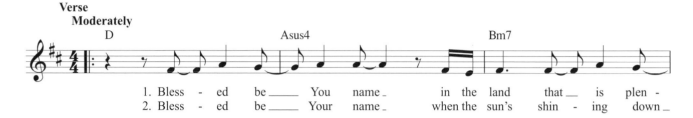

1. Bless - ed be ____ You name _ in the land that _ is plen -
2. Bless - ed be ____ Your name _ when the sun's shin - ing down _

- ti - ful, ___ where Your streams of ___ a - bun - dance flow, _ bless-ed be Your name.
___ on me, ___ when the world's all ___ as it ___ should be, ___ bless-ed be Your name.

Bless - ed be ____ Your name _ when I'm found in ____ the des -
Bless - ed be ____ Your name _ on the road marked _ with suf -

- ert place, _ though I walk through _ the wil - der - ness, _ bless-ed be Your name.
- fer - ing, ___ though there's pain in ____ the of - fer - ing, _ bless-ed be Your name.

Pre-Chorus

Ev - 'ry bless - ing You pour out I'll turn back to praise.

When the dark - ness clos - es in, Lord, _ still I will say: Bless-ed be the

Chorus

name of ___ the ___ Lord, ___ bless-ed be Your name. Bless-ed be the name of ___ the ___ Lord, ___

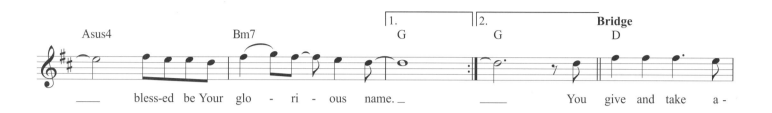

Bridge

___ bless-ed be Your glo - ri - ous name. ___ You give and take a -

To Coda

way. You give and take a - way. ___ My heart will choose to say, "Lord, bless-ed be Your

Pre-Chorus

name." ___ Ev-'ry bless-ing You pour out I'll ___ turn back to praise.

Chorus

When the dark-ness clos-es in, Lord, ___ still I'm gon-na say: ___ Bless-ed be the name of ___ the ___ Lord, ___

___ bless-ed be Your name, Je - sus. Bless-ed the the name of ___ the ___ Lord, ___ bless-ed be Your

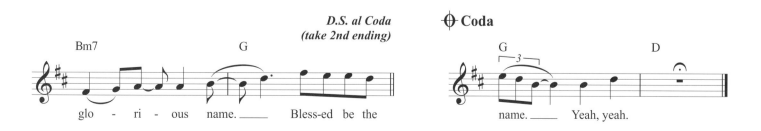

D.S. al Coda
(take 2nd ending)

Coda

glo - ri - ous name. ___ Bless-ed be the name. ___ Yeah, yeah.

The Blessing

Words and Music by Kari Jobe Carnes, Cody Carnes, Steven Furtick and Chris Brown

Build My Life

Words and Music by Matt Redman, Pat Barrett, Brett Younker, Karl Martin and Kirby Kaple

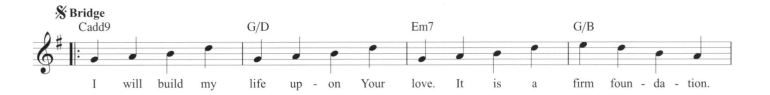

§ Bridge

I will build my life up-on Your love. It is a firm foun-da-tion.

To Coda ⊕

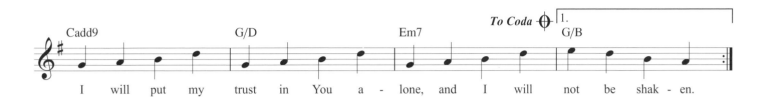

I will put my trust in You a-lone, and I will not be shak-en.

Chorus

not be shak-en. Ho-ly, there is no one like You, there is none be-

side You. O-pen up my eyes in won-der. And show me who You are, and

2nd time, D.S. al Coda

fill me with Your heart, and lead me in Your love to those a-round me.

⊕ Coda

Outro

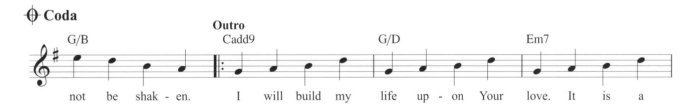

not be shak-en. I will build my life up-on Your love. It is a

firm foun-da-tion. I will put my trust in You a-

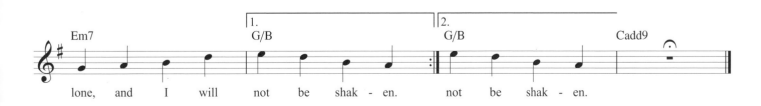

lone, and I will not be shak-en. not be shak-en.

Build Your Kingdom Here

Words and Music by Rend Collective

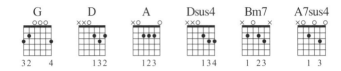

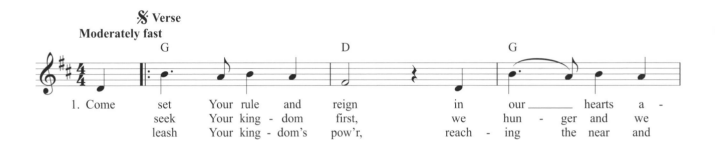

1. Come set Your rule and reign in our _____ hearts a-
seek Your king- dom first, we hun- ger and we
leash Your king- dom's pow'r, reach- ing the near and

gain. In- crease in us, we pray. Un- veil _____ why we're
thirst, re- fuse to waste our lives, for You're our joy and
far. No force of hell can stop Your beau- ty chang- ing

made. Come set our hearts a- blaze with hope, like wild- fire in our
prize. To see the cap- tive hearts re- leased; the hurt, the sick, the
hearts. You made us for much more than this; a- wake the king- dom

ver- y souls. Ho- ly Spir- it, come in- vade us now. _____
poor at peace, we lay down our lives for heav- en's cause. _____
seed in us. Fill us with the strength and love of Christ. _____

We are Your Church. We need Your pow'r in
We are Your Church. We pray: Re - vive this
We are Your Church. We are the hope on

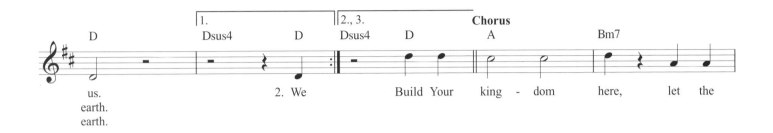

1. | 2., 3. | **Chorus**

us. 2. We
earth.
earth.

Build Your king - dom here, let the

dark - ness fear. Show Your might - y ___ hand, heal our streets and

land. _ Set Your Church on fire, win this na - tion back. Change the

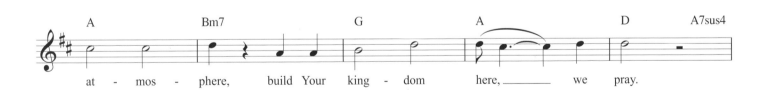

at - mos - phere, build Your king - dom here, ___ we pray.

To Coda *D.S. al Coda (take 2nd ending)* **Coda**

3. Un -

Cornerstone

Words and Music by Jonas Myrin, Reuben Morgan, Eric Liljero and Edward Mote

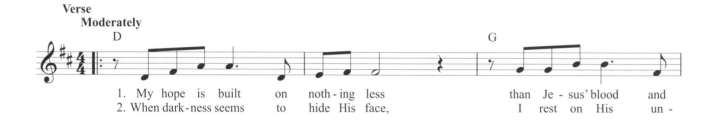

Verse
Moderately

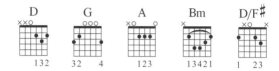

1. My hope is built on noth-ing less than Je-sus' blood and
2. When dark-ness seems to hide His face, I rest on His un-

right-eous-ness. I dare not trust the sweet-est frame, but whol-ly trust in Je -
chang-ing grace. In ev-'ry high and storm-y gale, my an-chor holds with-in ___

- sus' name. } **Chorus**
___ the veil. } Christ a - lone, Cor - ner - stone, weak made strong in the Sav - ior's

To Coda 1. 2.

love. Through the storm He is Lord, Lord of all. He is Lord,

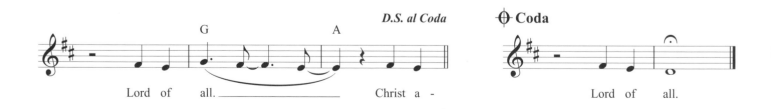

D.S. al Coda **Coda**

Lord of all. ___ Christ a - Lord of all.

Forever

Words and Music by Chris Tomlin

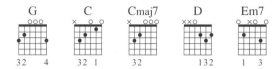

Verse
Moderately fast

1. Give thanks to the Lord, our God and King. His love en-dures for-ev-
2. With a might-y hand and out-stretched arm, His love en-dures for-ev-
3. From the ris-ing to the set-ting sun, His love en-dures for-ev-

-er. For He is good, He is a-bove all things. His
-er. For the life that's been re-born, His
-er. And by the grace of God we will car-ry on. His

love en-dures for-ev-er.
love en-dures for-ev-er.
love en-dures for-ev-er.

Sing praise, sing praise.

Sing praise, sing praise. For-ev-

Chorus

-er God is faith-ful, for-ev-er God is strong, for-ev-

-er God is with us, for-ev-er,

To Coda / *D.S. al Coda (take 2nd ending)* / *Coda*

for-ev-er.

Days of Elijah

Words and Music by Robin Mark

Everlasting God

Words and Music by Brenton Brown and Ken Riley

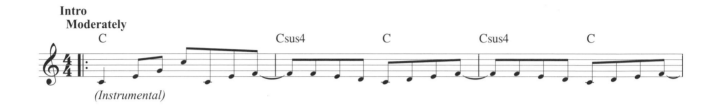

Intro
Moderately

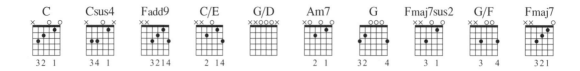

(Instrumental)

Verse

1., 2. Strength will rise as we wait ___ up - on the Lord, we will wait ___

___ up - on the Lord, we will wait ___ up - on the Lord. Strength will rise as we wait ___

___ up - on the Lord, we will wait ___ up - on the Lord, we will wait ___ up - on the Lord. Our God, ___

Pre-Chorus

___ You reign ___ for - ev - er. Our hope, ___ our Strong ___ De - liv-

Chorus

- er - er. You are ___ the ev - er - last - ing God, ___ the ev-

-er - last - ing God. ___ You do ___ not faint, _ You ___ won't grow wea - ry.

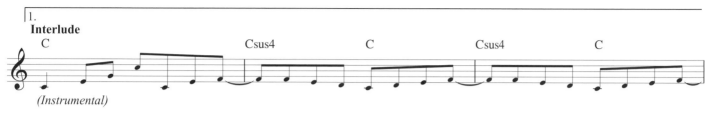

1.
Interlude

(Instrumental)

2.
Chorus

You're the ___ de - fend - er of ___ the weak. ___ You com-

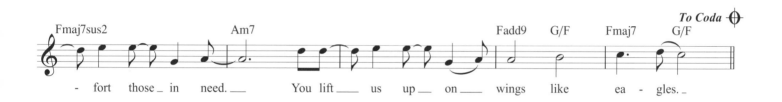

To Coda

-fort those _ in need. ___ You lift ___ us up ___ on ___ wings like ea - gles. _

D.S. al Coda
(take 2nd ending)

Interlude

(Instrumental)

Our God, _

Coda
Outro

From ev - er - last - ing to ev - er - last - ing,

God, You are ev - er - last - ing. *(Instrumental)*

rit.

Glorious Day

Words and Music by Sean Curran, Kristian Stanfill, Jason Ingram and Jonathan Smith

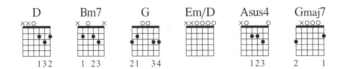

Verse
Moderately

1. I was bur - ied __ be - neath __ my shame. __ Who could

car - ry __ that kind __ of weight? __ It was my tomb

till I met You. 2. I was breath - ing, __ but not __ a - live. __
mer - cy __ has saved __ my soul. __

All my fail - ures I tried __ to hide. __
Now Your free - dom __ is all __ that I know. __

It was my tomb till I met You. ⎬ You called my
The old made new, Je - sus, when I met You. ⎭

Chorus

name,_____ and I ran out of that _ grave, _ out of the dark - ness _ in-

to Your glo - ri - ous _ day. ____ You called my name, _____ and

I ran out of that _ grave, __ out of the dark - ness _ in-

to Your glo - ri - ous _ day. ____ 3. Now Your

2. **Bridge**

I need - ed res - cue. My sin was heav - y. But chains break at the

weight of Your glo - ry. I need - ed shel - ter. I was an or - phan. Now You call me a

cit - i - zen of heav - en.   When I was bro - ken,   You were my heal - ing.   Now Your love is the

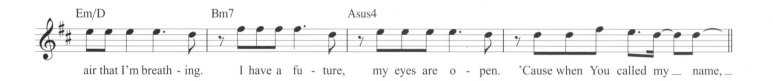

air that I'm breath - ing.   I have a fu - ture,   my eyes are o - pen.   'Cause when You called my ___ name, ___

Chorus

___   I ran out of that ___ grave, ___   out of the

dark - ness ___ in - to Your glo - ri - ous ___ day. ___   You called my

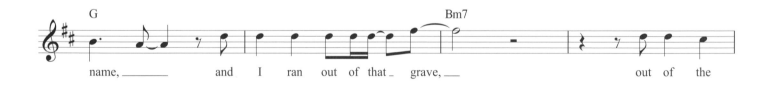

name, _____   and I ran out of that ___ grave, ___   out of the

dark - ness ___ in - to Your glo - ri - ous ___ day. ___

Goodness of God

Words and Music by Ben Fielding, Ed Cash, Jason Ingram, Jenn Johnson and Brian Johnson

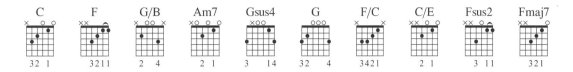

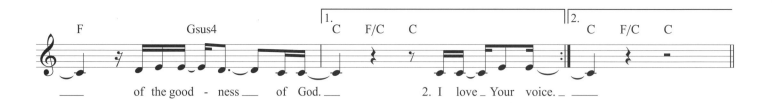

of the good - ness ___ of God. ___   2. I love ___ Your voice. ___

Bridge

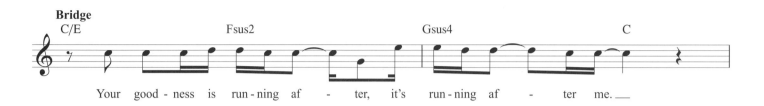

Your good - ness is run - ning af - ter, it's run - ning af - ter me. ___

Your good - ness is run - ning af - ter, it's run - ning af - ter me. ___ With my life ___

___ laid down, _ I'm sur - ren - dered now. _ I give ___ You ev - 'ry - thing, _____

'cause Your goood - ness is run - ning af - ter, it's run - ning af - ter me. ___

Chorus

All my life ___ You have _ been faith - ful.   All my life ___ You have _ been so,

___ so ___ good.   With ev - 'ry breath _ that I ___ am a - ble,   oh, I'm _ gon - na sing _

Chorus

___ of the good - ness ___ of God. ___   All my life ___ You have _ been faith -

- ful. And all my life __ You have __ been so, _____ so good.

With ev - 'ry breath __ that I _____ am a - ble, oh, I'm __ gon - na sing __

_____ of the good - ness _____ of God. _____ Oh, I'm __ gon - na sing __

_____ of the good - ness _____ of God. _____

God Is Able

Words and Music by Reuben Morgan and Ben Fielding

Verse

Moderately

G

1. God is a-ble, __ He will nev-er __ fail. __
with __ us, __ God is on our __ side.

D

Em

He is Al-might-y __ God. __ Great-er than all we __ seek, __ great-er than
He will __ make __ a way. __ Far __ a-bove all we __ know, __ far __ a-bove

C

G

D

Em

Cmaj7

D

all we __ ask, __ He has done __ great __ things. __
all we __ hope, __ He has done __ great __ things. __

Lift-ed up, __

Chorus

G

D

Em

__ He de-feat-ed the grave. __ Raised to life, __ our God is a-

C

G

D

-ble. In His Name, __ we o-ver-come, __ for the Lord __

Em

D7

C

__ our God is a- ble. __

1.

G

D

2.

Interlude

Em

C

G

D

2. God is (Instrumental)

Bridge

God is with us, ___ He will

go be - fore. He will nev - er leave us. ___ He will nev - er leave us. ___ God is

for us. ___ He has o - pen ___ arms. He will nev - er fail us. ___ He will nev - er

Chorus

fail us. ___ Lif - ted up, _____ He de-feat - ed the grave. ___ Raised to life, ___

___ our God is a - ble. In His Name, ___ we o - ver - come ___

1.

___ for the Lord ___ our God is a - ble. Lift - ed up,

2.

Outro

- ble, for the Lord ___ our God is a - ble, for the Lord ___

___ our God is a - ble. _____

God of Wonders

Words and Music by Marc Byrd and Steve Hindalong

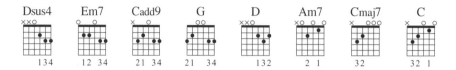

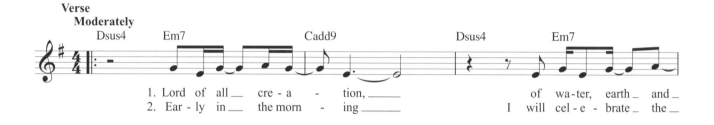

Verse
Moderately

Dsus4   Em7   Cadd9   Dsus4   Em7

1. Lord of all ___ cre - a - tion, _____ of wa-ter, earth ___ and _
2. Ear - ly in ___ the morn - ing _____ I will cel - e - brate ___ the _

Cadd9   Dsus4   Em7   Cadd9

___ sky, _____ the heav - ens are Your tab - er - na - cle; _____
___ light. _____ And as I stum - ble in the dark - ness, _____

Dsus4   Em7   Cadd9   **Chorus**   G

glo - ry to the Lord ___ on _____ high. _____ God of won - ders be-yond our gal - ax -
I will call Your name ___ by _____ night. _____

D   Am7   Cmaj7

y, You are ho - ly, ___ ho - ly. ___ The

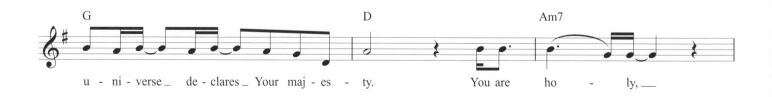

G   D   Am7

u - ni - verse ___ de - clares Your maj - es - ty. You are ho - ly, ___

ho - ly, __ Lord of heav-en and __ earth, __ Lord of heav-en and __ earth. __

Outro

__ Hal - le - lu - jah __ to the Lord of __ heav-en and __ earth. __

__ Hal - le - lu - jah __ to the Lord of __ heav - en and __ earth. __

__ Hal - le - lu - jah __ to the Lord of __ heav-en and __ earth. __

Good Good Father

Words and Music by Pat Barrett and Anthony Brown

Great Are You Lord

Words and Music by Jason Ingram, David Leonard and Leslie Jordan

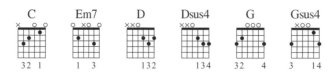

Verse
Moderately slow, in 2

1. You give (2.) life, You are love, You bring light to _____ the

dark - ness. You give hope, You re - store ev - 'ry heart that is

bro - ken. And great are You, ___ Lord. ___ It's Your

Chorus

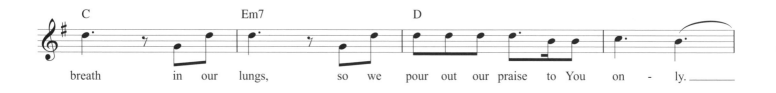

breath in our lungs, so we pour out our praise, we pour out our praise. It's Your

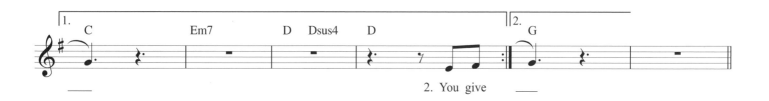

breath in our lungs, so we pour out our praise to You on - ly. ___

2. You give _____

Bridge

All the earth will shout Your praise. Our hearts will cry, these

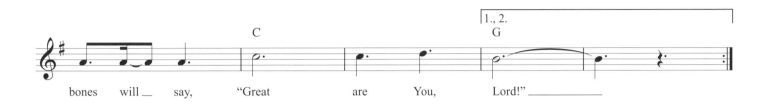

bones will say, "Great are You, Lord!" _____

3.

Lord!" _____ It's Your breath in our lungs, so we

Chorus

pour out our praise, we pour out our praise. It's Your breath in our

1.

lungs, so we pour out our praise to You on - ly. It's Your

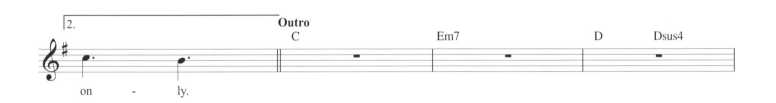

2. **Outro**

on - ly.

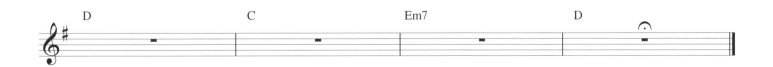

The Heart of Worship
(When the Music Fades)

Words and Music by Matt Redman

Verse
Moderately

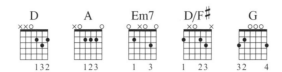

1. When the mu - sic fades, _____ all is stripped a - way,
2. King of end - less worth, _____ no one could ex - press _____

and I sim - ply come, _____ long - ing just to bring _____
how much You de - serve. _____ Though I'm weak and poor, _____

some - thing that's of worth _____ that will bless Your heart. _____
all I have is Yours, _____ ev - 'ry sin - gle breath. _____

Pre-Chorus

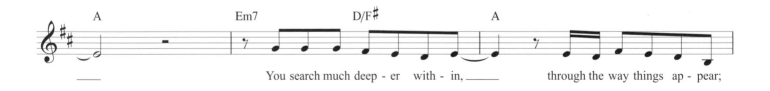

I'll bring You more than a song, _____ for a song in it - self is not what You have re - quired. _____

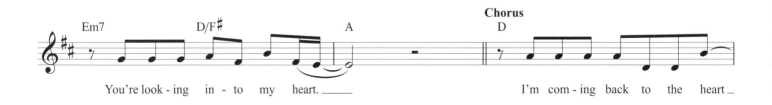

You search much deep - er with - in, _____ through the way things ap - pear;

Chorus

You're look - ing in - to my heart. _____ I'm com - ing back to the heart _____

of wor - ship, and it's all a - bout _ You, _ all a - bout _ You, _ Je - sus.

I'm sor - ry, Lord, for the thing ___ I've made _ it, when it's all a - bout _ You, _

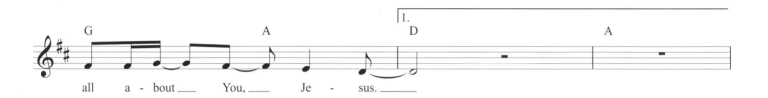

all a - bout ___ You, ___ Je - sus. _____

Here I Am to Worship
(Light of the World)

Words and Music by Tim Hughes

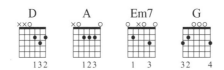

Verse
Moderately slow

1. Light of the world, You stepped down in-to dark - ness, o - pened my eyes, let me see
2. King of all days, oh, so high - ly ex - alt - ed, glo - rious in heav - en a - bove,

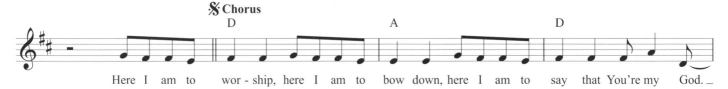

beau - ty that made this __ heart a - dore You, hope of a life spent with You.
hum - bly You came to the earth You cre - at - ed, all for love's sake be - came poor.

% Chorus

Here I am to wor - ship, here I am to bow down, here I am to say that You're my God. __

To Coda ⊕

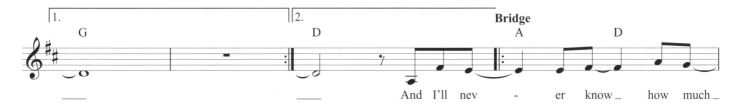

__ You're al - to-geth - er love - ly, al - to-geth - er wor - thy, al - to-geth - er won - der - ful to me. __

1. / 2. **Bridge**

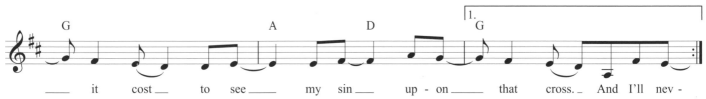

__ And I'll nev - er know __ how much __

1. / 2. **D.S. al Coda** ⊕ **Coda**

__ it cost __ to see __ my sin __ up - on __ that cross. __ And I'll nev -

__ that cross. __ Here I am to

__

In Christ Alone

Words and Music by Keith Getty and Stuart Townend

Holy Is the Lord

Words and Music by Chris Tomlin and Louie Giglio

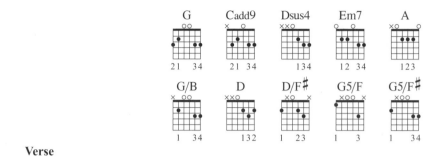

Verse
Moderately

1., 2. We stand and lift up our hands, for the joy of the Lord is our strength.
*Substitute G/B on 2nd verse.

We bow down and wor - ship Him now. How great,

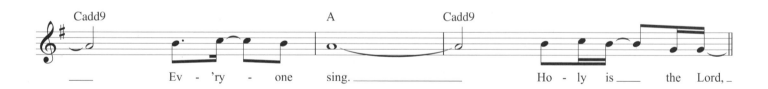

how awe - some is He. And to - geth - er we sing.
**As before

Pre-Chorus

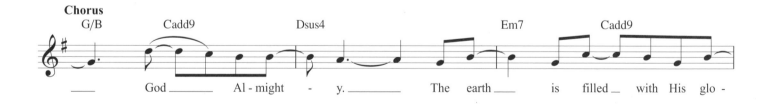

Ev - 'ry - one sing. Ho - ly is the Lord,

Chorus

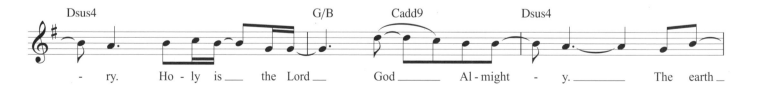

God Al - might - y. The earth is filled with His glo - ry. Ho - ly is the Lord God Al - might - y. The earth

Holy Spirit

Words and Music by Katie Torwalt and Bryan Torwalt

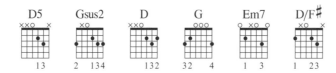

1., 2. There's noth - ing worth more ____ that could ev - er come close ____

____ No - thing can com - pare; ____ You're our liv - ing hope. ____

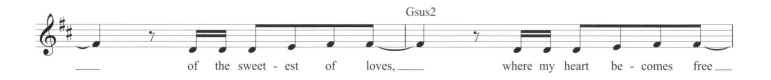

Your pres - ence, ____ Lord. I've tast - ed and seen ____

____ of the sweet - est of loves, ____ where my heart be - comes free ____

____ and my shame is un - done. ____ Your pres - ence, ____

Chorus

____ Lord. Ho - ly Spir - it, You are wel - come here. Come

flood this place and fill the at - mos - phere. Your glo - ry, God, is what our

hearts long for, to be o - ver - come by Your pres - ence, Lord. _____

_____ Your pres - ence, _____ Lord.

Bridge

Let us ____ be - come _ more a - ware ____ of Your pres - ence. _

Play 4 times

Let us ____ ex - pe - ri - ence _ the glo - ry of ____ Your good - ness. _

Outro-Chorus

Ho - ly Spir - it, You are wel - come here. Come

flood this place and fill the at - mos - phere. Your glo - ry, God, is what our

hearts long for, to be o - ver - come by Your pres - ence, Lord. _____

Hosanna
(Praise Is Rising)

Words and Music by Paul Baloche and Brenton Brown

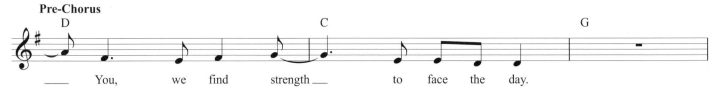

In Your pres - ence, all our fears ____ are washed a - way,

washed a - way. ____ Ho - san -

Chorus

na, ho - san - na. ____ You are the God ____

____ who saves us, ____ wor - thy of all ____ our prais - es. ____

____ Ho - san - na, ho - san - na. ____

____ Come have Your way ____ a - mong us. ____ We wel - come You here, ____

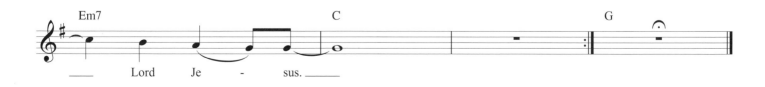

____ Lord Je - sus. ____

How Great Is Our God

Words and Music by Chris Tomlin, Jesse Reeves and Ed Cash

Verse
Moderately slow

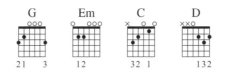

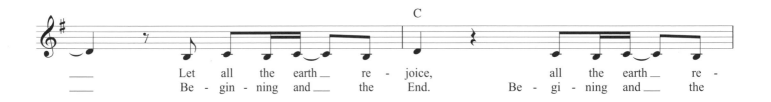

1. The splen - dor of ___ a King, ___ clothed in maj - es - ty. ___
age to age ___ He stands, ___ and time is in ___ His hands.

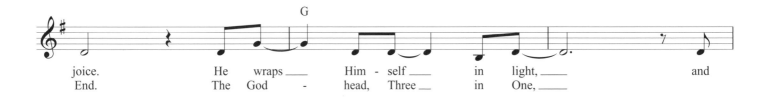

Let all the earth ___ re - joice, all the earth ___ re -
Be - gin - ning and ___ the End. Be - gi - ning and ___ the

joice. He wraps ___ Him - self ___ in light, ___ and
End. The God - head, Three ___ in One, ___

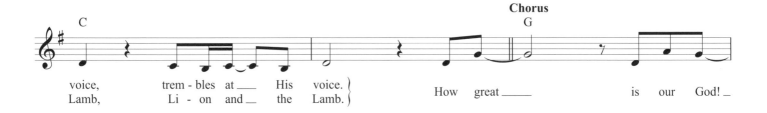

dark - ness tries ___ to hide. ___ It trem - bles at ___ His
Fa - ther, Spir - it, Son, ___ the Li - on and ___ the

Chorus

voice, trem - bles at ___ His voice. }   How great ___ is our God! ___
Lamb, Li - on and ___ the Lamb. }

Sing with me, ___ how great is our God! ___ And all ___ will see how

great,   how   great ___   is   our   God! ___   2. And

Bridge

Name   a - bove _____   all   names,

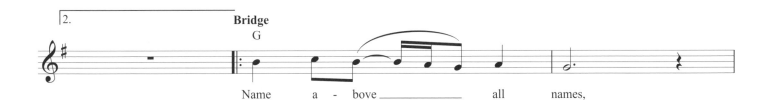

wor - thy   of _____   all   praise.   My   heart   will   sing, ___   "How   great __

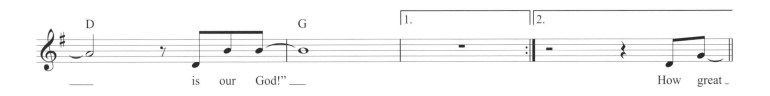

___   is   our   God!" ___   How   great _

Chorus

___   is   our   God! ___   Sing   with   me, _   how   great   is   our   God! _

___   And   all ___   will   see   how   great,   how   great ___   is   our   God! _

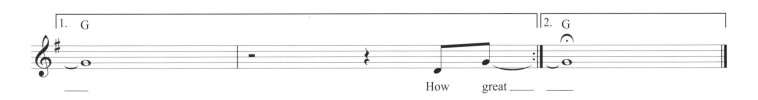

___   How   great ___ ___

Jesus Messiah

Words and Music by Chris Tomlin, Jesse Reeves, Daniel Carson and Ed Cash

-ners, _____ the ran - some from heav - en. _____

To Coda ⊕

Je - sus Mes - si - ah, _____ Lord of all. _____

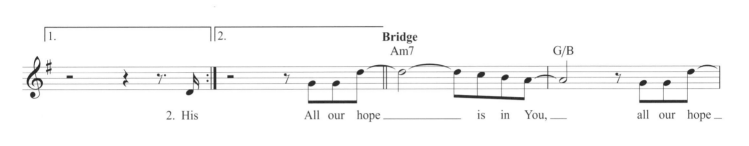

2. His

All our hope _____ is in You, _____ all our hope _____

_____ is in You. _____ All the glo - ry to You, _

_____ God, _____ the Light of _____ the world.

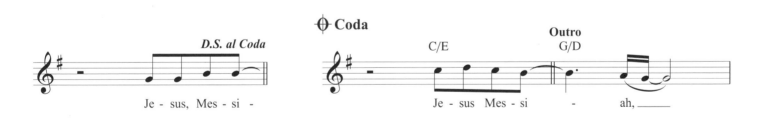

⊕ **Coda**

Outro

D.S. al Coda

Je - sus, Mes - si -

Je - sus Mes - si - ah, _____

Lord of all. _____ You're the Lord _____ of all, _____

_____ the Lord _____ of all. _____

King of Kings

Words and Music by Scott Ligertwood, Brooke Ligertwood and Jason Ingram

The Lion and the Lamb

Words and Music by Brenton Brown, Brian Johnson and Leeland Mooring

Verse

Slow

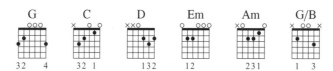

1. He's com-ing on the clouds; kings and king-doms will bow down. _____
   o-pen up the gates, make way be-fore the King of Kings. _____

_____ And ev-'ry chain will break as bro-ken hearts de-clare His praise.)
_____ Our God who comes to save is here to set the cap-tives free.)
Well, who can stop the

%Chorus

Lord Al-might-y? Our God is _____ the Li-on, _____ the Li-on _____ of

Ju-dah, _____ He's roar-ing _____ with pow-er _____ and fight-ing _____ our bat-tles. And ev-'ry knee will

bow be-fore Him. Our God is _____ the Lamb, _____ the Lamb that _____ was

slain ___ for the sin of ___ the world. _____ His blood breaks _ the chains, and ev - 'ry knee will

To Coda ⊕

bow be-fore the Li - on and the Lamb. Oh, ev - 'ry knee will bow be-fore the Li - on and the

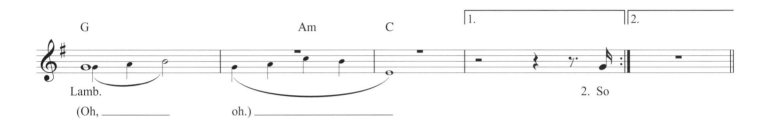

1.   2.

Lamb.

(Oh, _____ oh.) _____ 2. So

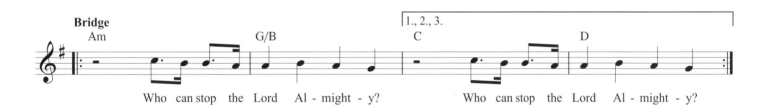

Bridge   1., 2., 3.

Who can stop the Lord Al - might - y?   Who can stop the Lord Al - might - y?

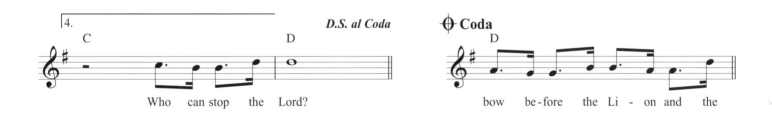

4.   *D.S. al Coda*   ⊕ **Coda**

Who can stop the Lord?   bow be-fore the Li - on and the

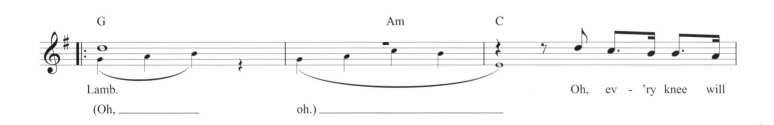

Lamb.

(Oh, _____ oh.) _____ Oh, ev - 'ry knee will

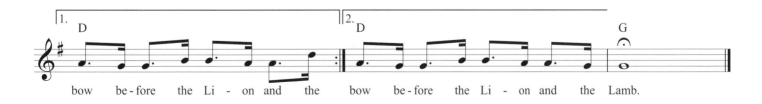

1.   2.

bow be-fore the Li - on and the   bow be-fore the Li - on and the Lamb.

Living Hope

Words and Music by Phil Wickham and Brian Johnson

Lord, I Lift Your Name on High

Words and Music by Rick Founds

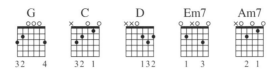

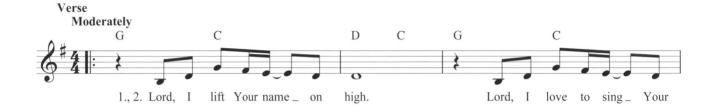

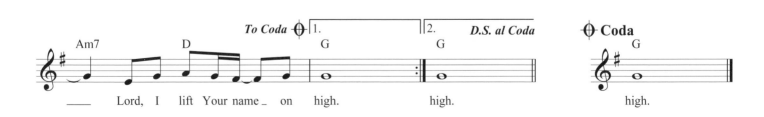

Lord, I Need You

Words and Music by Jesse Reeves, Kristian Stanfill, Matt Maher, Christy Nockels and Daniel Carson

Mighty to Save

Words and Music by Ben Fielding and Reuben Morgan

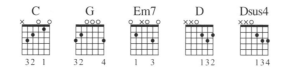

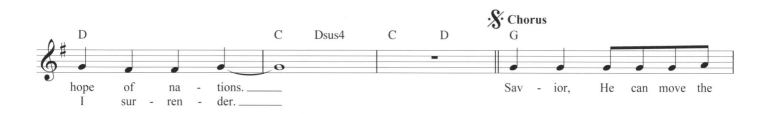

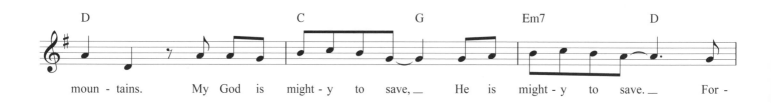

ev - er Au - thor of sal - va - tion. He rose and con-quered the grave,_ Je - sus

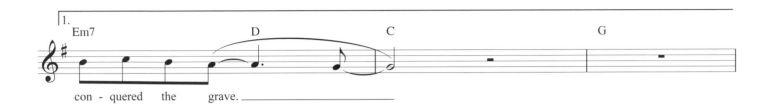

con - quered the grave. _____

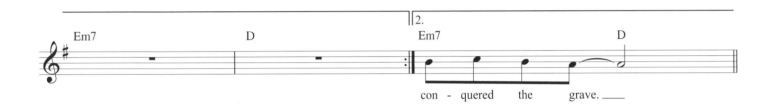

con - quered the grave. ____

Bridge

Shine your light and _____ let the whole world _____ see we're sing - ing

for the glo - ry _____ of the ris - en _____ King, _____ Je - sus.

Shine your light and _____ let the whole world _____ see we're sing - ing

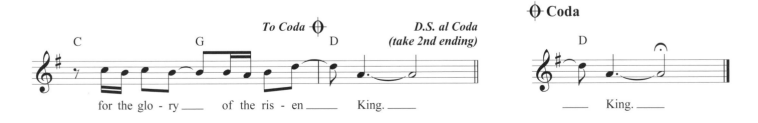

for the glo - ry _____ of the ris - en _____ King. _____   _____ King. ____

O Come to the Altar

Words and Music by Chris Brown, Mack Brock, Steven Furtick and Wade Joye

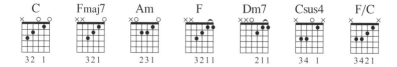

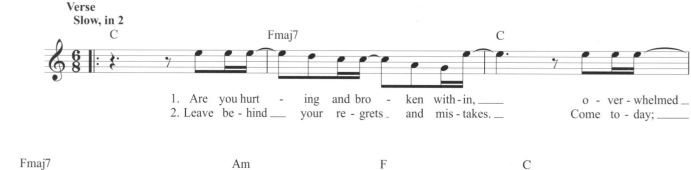

Verse
Slow, in 2

1. Are you hurt - ing and bro - ken with - in, _____ o - ver - whelmed
2. Leave be - hind _____ your re - grets _ and mis - takes. _____ Come to - day; _____

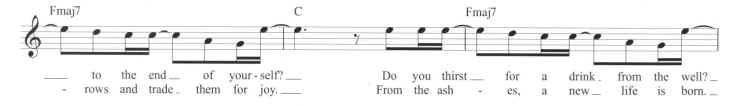

_____ by the weight _ of your sin? _____ Je - sus is call - ing. _ Have you come _
_____ there's no rea - son to wait. _____ Je - sus is call - ing. _ Bring your sor -

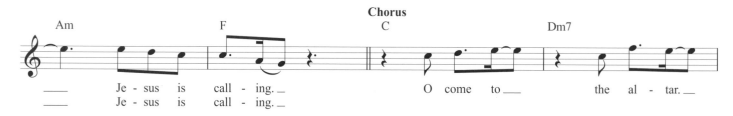

_____ to the end _ of your - self? _____ Do you thirst _ for a drink _ from the well?
- rows and trade _ them for joy. _____ From the ash - es, a new _ life is born.

Chorus

_____ Je - sus is call - ing. _ O come to _____ the al - tar. _
_____ Je - sus is call - ing. _

The Fa - ther's _ arms are _ o - pen _ wide. _____ For - give - ness _ was bought with _

the pre - cious _ blood of _____ Je - sus _____ Christ.

O Praise the Name
(Anastasis)

Words and Music by Marty Sampson, Benjamin Hastings and Dean Ussher

Reckless Love

Words and Music by Caleb Culver, Cory Asbury and Ran Jackson

Verse
Slow, in 2

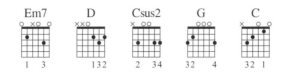

1. Be - fore I spoke a word, ___ You were sing - ing o - ver me.
2. When I was Your foe, ___ still Your love ___ fought ___ for me.

You have been ___ so, so ___ good ___ to me. ___
You have been ___ so, so ___ good ___ to me. ___

Be - fore I took a breath, ___ You breathed Your ___
When I felt no worth, ___ You paid all ___

___ life in me. You have been ___
___ for me. You have been ___

so, so ___ kind ___ to me. ___ }
so, so ___ kind ___ to me. ___ }
Oh, the

𝄋 Chorus

o - ver - whelm - ing, ___ nev - er - end - ing, ___ reck - less ___ love of God. ___

Oh, it chas - es ___ me down, ___ fights till ___ I'm found, ___

leaves the nine - ty - nine. ___ I could-n't earn ___ it, and I don't de - serve ___

___ it, still You ___ give Your - self a - way. ___ Oh, the

1.

o - ver - whelm - ing, ___ nev - er - end - ing, ___ reck - less ___ love of God, ___

Interlude

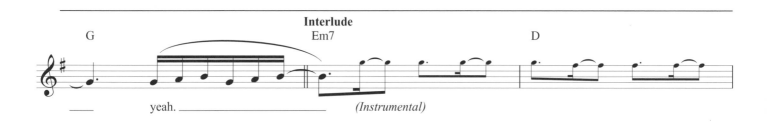

___ yeah. _____ *(Instrumental)*

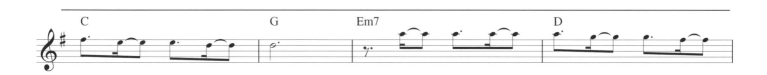

2.

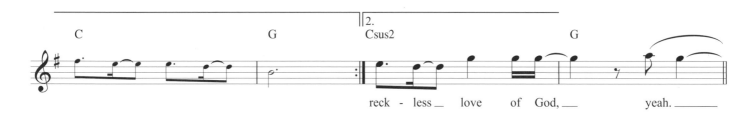

reck - less ___ love of God, ___ yeah. ___

Interlude

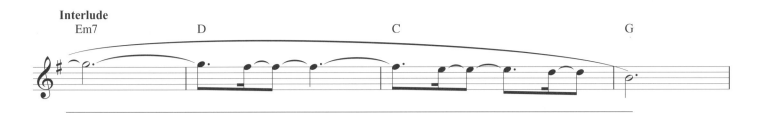

(Instrumental)

Bridge

There's no shad-ow You won't light up, moun-tain You won't climb up com-ing af-ter me.

There's no wall You won't kick down, lie You won't

tear down com-ing af-ter me. There's no shad-ow You won't

light up, moun-tain You won't climb up com-ing af-ter me.

D.S. al Fine
(take 2nd ending)

There's no wall You won't kick down, lie You won't tear down com-ing af-ter me. Oh, the

Oceans
(Where Feet May Fail)

Words and Music by Joel Houston, Matt Crocker and Salomon Lighthelm

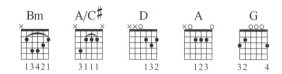

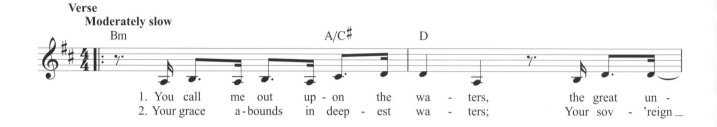

Verse
Moderately slow

1. You call me out up-on the wa-ters, the great un-
2. Your grace a-bounds in deep-est wa-ters; Your sov-'reign

- known where feet may __ fail. And there I find You in the
__ hand will be my __ guide. Where feet may fail and fear sur-

mys-t'ry; in o-ceans __ deep, my faith __ will __ stand.
rounds me, You've nev-er __ failed, and You won't __ start __ now.

Chorus

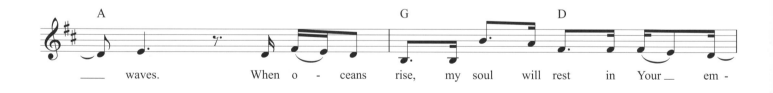

And I will call up-on __ Your __ name and keep my eyes a-bove __ the __

__ waves. When o-ceans rise, my soul will rest in Your __ em-

- brace, __ for I am Yours, You are __ mine.

Bridge

Spir - it, lead ___ me where ___ my trust ___

___ is with - out bor - ders. Let me walk ___ up - on ___ the wa - ters, wher-ev -

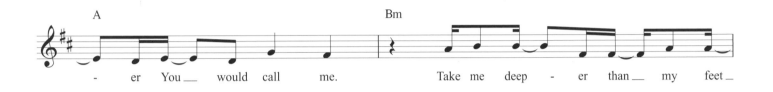

- er You ___ would call me. Take me deep - er than ___ my feet ___

___ could ev - er wan - der, and my faith ___ will be ___ made strong - er in the pres-

Outro-Chorus

- ence of ___ my Sav - ior. I will call up - on ___ Your ___ name.

Keep my eyes a - bove ___ the ___ waves. My soul will rest in Your ___ em-

- brace. I am Yours, and You are ___ mine.

One Thing Remains
(Your Love Never Fails)

Words and Music by Jeremy Riddle, Brian Johnson and Christa Black

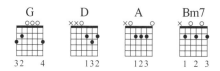

Verse
Moderately

1. High - er than the moun - tains that I _____ face,
on and on and on and on it _____ goes. Yes, it's

strong - er than the pow - er of the _____ grave,
o - ver-whelms and sat - is - fies my _____ soul. And I'll

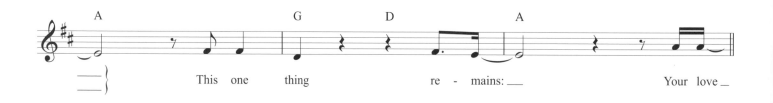

con - stant in the tri - al and the _____ change, this one thing re - mains. _____
nev - er ev - er have to be a - fraid, 'cause this one thing re - mains. _____

This one thing re - mains: _____ Your love _____

% Chorus

_____ nev - er fails, it nev - er gives up, it nev - er runs out on me. Your love _____

nev-er fails, it nev-er gives up, it nev-er runs out on me. Your love

nev-er fails, it nev-er gives up, it nev-er runs out on me, Your

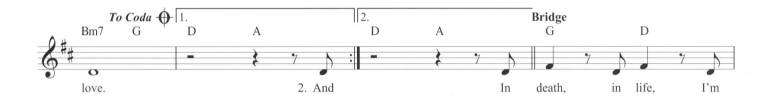

To Coda ⊕ | 1. | 2. | **Bridge**

love.   2. And   In death, in life, I'm

con - fi - dent and cov - ered by __ the pow'r of Your great love. My

debt is paid; there's noth - ing that can sep - a - rate __ my heart from Your great

D.S. al Coda   ⊕ **Coda**

love.   Your love __

Open the Eyes of My Heart

Words and Music by Paul Baloche

Open Up the Heavens

Words and Music by Jason Ingram, Stuart Garrard,
Andi Rozier, James MacDonald and Meredith Andrews

Verse
Moderately

1. We wait-ed for this day, we're gath-ered in Your ___ name,
pres-ence in this place, Your glo-ry on our ___ face, we're

call-ing out to ___ You. ___ Your glo-ry like a fire, a-
look-ing to the ___ sky. ___ De-scend-ing like a cloud, You're

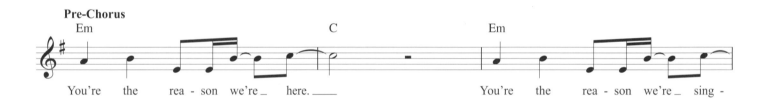

wak-en-ing de-sire, will burn our hearts with ___ truth. ___
stand-ing with us ___ now. Lord, un-veil our ___ eyes. ___

Pre-Chorus

You're the rea-son we're ___ here. ___ You're the rea-son we're ___ sing-

Chorus

- ing. ___ O-pen up the heav-ens; ___ we wan-na see You. ___

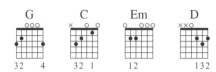

O-pen up the flood-gates, ___ a might-y riv-er ___ flow-ing from Your heart,

Our God

Words and Music by Jonas Myrin, Jesse Reeves, Chris Tomlin and Matt Redman

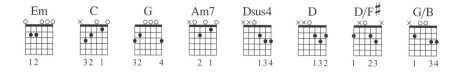

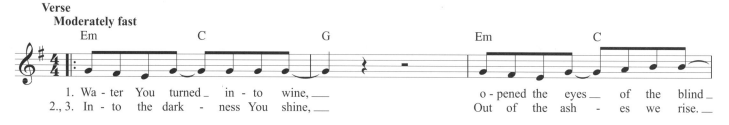

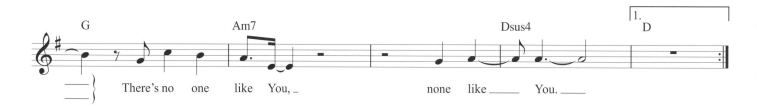

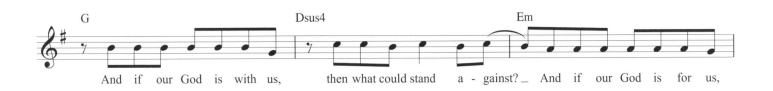

And if our God is with us, then what could stand a - gainst? _ And if our God is for us,

then who could ev - er stop us? And if our God is with us, then what could stand a - gainst? _

_ sim.

What could stand a - gainst? _

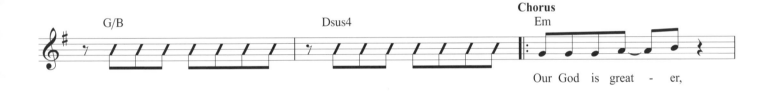

Chorus

Our God is great - er,

Our God is strong - er, God, You are high - er than an - y oth - er.

Our God is Heal - er, awe-some in pow - er, our _ God, _ our _ God. _

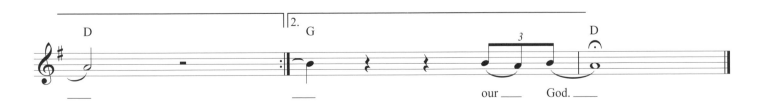

our _ God. _ our _ God. _

Revelation Song

Words and Music by Jennie Lee Riddle

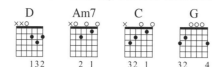

Verse
Moderately slow

1. Wor - thy is the Lamb who was slain. Ho - ly, ho - ly is ___ He. ___

___ Sing a new song to Him who sits on

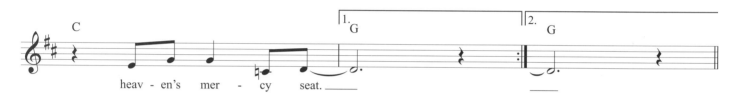

heav - en's mer - cy seat. ___

Chorus

Ho - ly, ho - ly, ho - ly is the ___ Lord God ___ Al - might - y,

who was ___ and is ___ and is ___ to come. ___

With all cre - a - tion I ___ sing praise to the King of kings. ___

You are my ev - 'ry - thing, ___ and I will ___ a - dore You. ___

Verse
To Coda

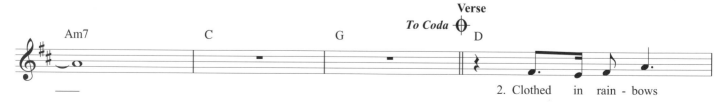

___ 2. Clothed in rain - bows

Shout to the Lord

Words and Music by Darlene Zschech

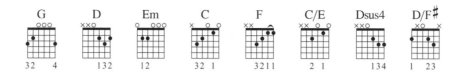

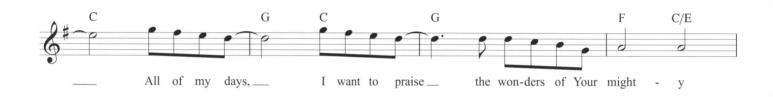

1., 2. My Je - sus, my Sav - ior; Lord, there is none __ like You. __

All of my days, __ I want to praise __ the won-ders of Your might - y

love. My com - fort, my shel - ter, Tow - er of ref - uge and strength; __

__ let ev-'ry breath, __ all that I am, __ nev - er cease to wor - ship You.

Shout to the Lord, __ all the earth, __ let us sing; Pow - er and maj - es - ty, praise __

_____ to the King! _____ Moun-tains bow down _ and the sea _____ will roar _ at the

sound _ of Your name. _____ I sing for joy _ at the work _ of Your hands, _ for -

ev - er I'll love _ You, for - ev - er I'll stand. _ Noth-ing com - pares _ to the prom -

- ise I have _ in You. _   - ise I have _ in...

Coda

- ise I have _ in... Noth-ing com - pares _ to the prom - ise I have _ in...

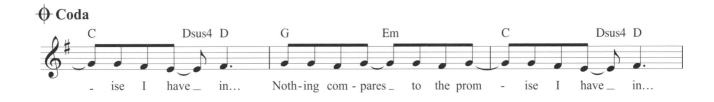

Noth-ing com - pares _ to the prom - ise I have _ in You. _____

This Is Amazing Grace

Words and Music by Phil Wickham, Joshua Neil Farro and Jeremy Riddle

Verse
Moderately

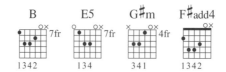

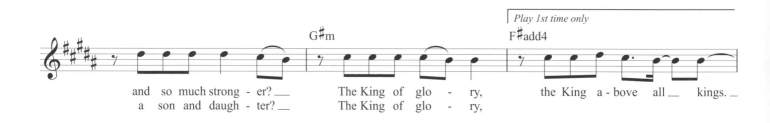

and so much strong - er? __ The King of glo - ry, the King a - bove all __ kings. __
a son and daugh - ter? __ The King of glo - ry,

Play 2nd time only

__ the King of glo - ry.

Who shakes the whole earth
Who rules the na - tions

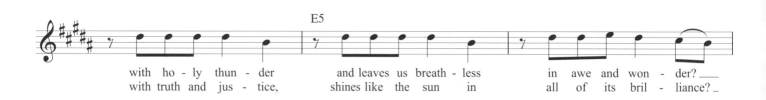

with ho - ly thun - der and leaves us breath - less in awe and won - der? __
with truth and jus - tice, shines like the sun in all of its bril - liance? __

The King of glo - ry, the King a - bove all __ kings. __ This is a - maz - ing __ grace,

Chorus

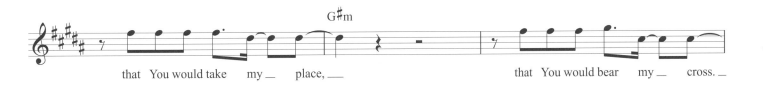

this is un-fail-ing __ love, _____

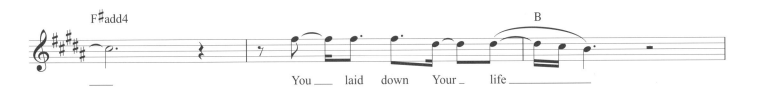

that You would take my __ place, __   that You would bear my __ cross. __

You __ laid down Your __ life _____

that I would be set free. _____   Oh, __

To Coda ⊕

Je - sus, I sing __ for   all that You've done for __ me. __

Bridge

Wor - thy is the Lamb who was slain. __   Wor - thy is the King who con -

- quered the grave. _

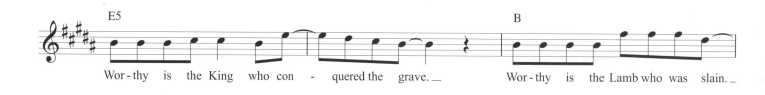

Wor - thy is the Lamb who was slain. __

Wor - thy is the King who con - quered the grave. _   Wor - thy is the Lamb who was slain. _

___   Wor - thy is the King who con - quered the grave. _

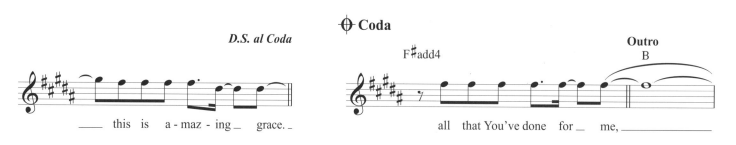

Wor - thy is the Lamb who was slain. _   Wor - thy, wor - thy, wor - thy! _ Oh, _

⊕ Coda

D.S. al Coda

F♯add4   **Outro**
B

__ this is a - maz - ing _ grace. _   all that You've done for _ me, _____

_____   all that You've done for _ me. _____

10,000 Reasons
(Bless the Lord)

Words and Music by Jonas Myrin and Matt Redman

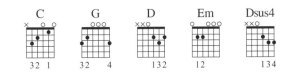

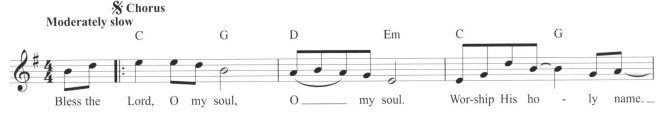

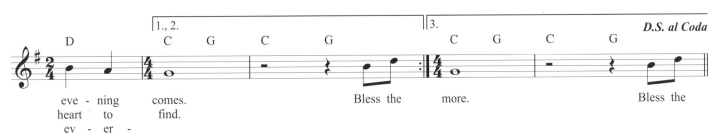

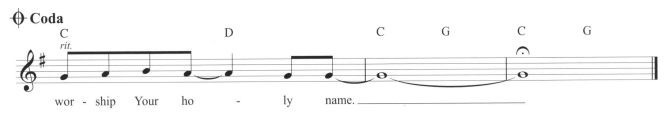

Way Maker

Words and Music by Osinachi Okoro

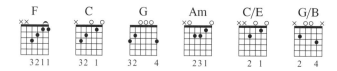

Verse

Moderately

1. You are here, _____ (2.) mov-ing in _____ our _____ midst. I wor-ship You,

_____ I wor-ship You. _____ You are here, _____ work-ing in _____ this _____

_____ place. I wor-ship You, _____ I wor-ship You. 2. You are here, _____

Chorus

_____ Way mak-er, mir-a-cle work-er, prom-ise keep-er, light in the dark-ness, _____

_____ my God, that is who You are. Way mak-er, mir-a-cle work-er,

To Coda

prom-ise keep-er, light in the dark-ness, _____ my God, that is who You are. 3. You are here, _____

Way mak - er, mir - a - cle work - er, prom - ise keep - er, light in the dark - ness, my God, that is who you

Outro

are. You are here, _____ touch - ing ev - 'ry _____ life. I wor - ship You, _

_____ I wor - ship You. _____ You are here, _____ meet - ing ev - 'ry _____

_____ need. I wor - ship You, _____ I wor - ship You. ___

We Fall Down

Words and Music by Chris Tomlin

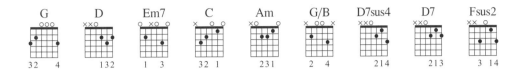

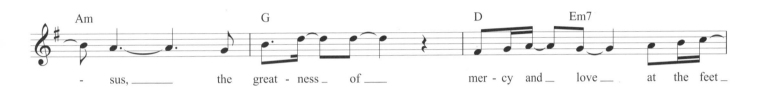

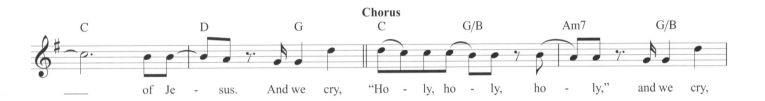

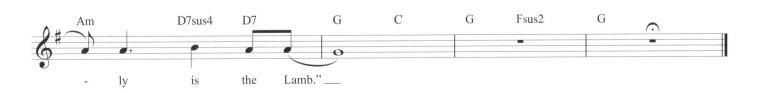

What a Beautiful Name

Words and Music by Ben Fielding and Brooke Ligertwood

Verse
Slow, in 2

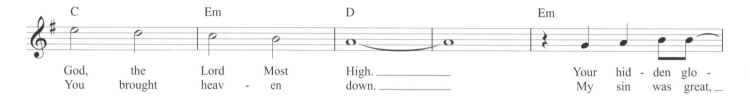

1. You were the Word at the be-gin-ning, one with
2. You did-n't want heav-en with-out us, so, Je-sus,

God, the Lord Most High. Your hid-den glo-
You brought heav-en down. My sin was great,

-ry in cre-a-tion, now re-vealed in You, our
Your love was great-er. What could sep-a-rate us

Chorus

Christ.)
now?) What a beau-ti-ful name it is, what a beau-ti-ful name it is,

the name of Je-sus Christ, my King. What a

beau-ti-ful name it is, noth-ing com-pares to this. What a

beau-ti-ful name it is, the name of Je-sus.

Who You Say I Am

Words and Music by Reuben Morgan and Ben Fielding

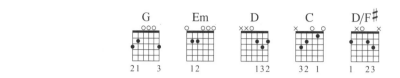

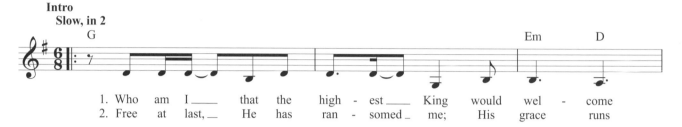

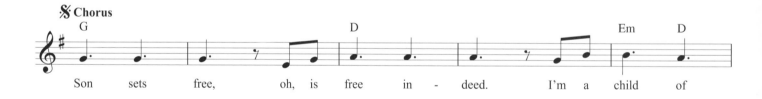

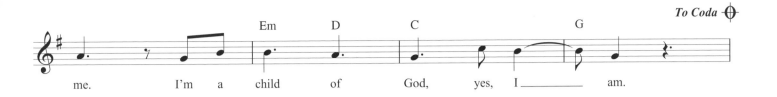

me. I'm a child of God, yes, I_____ am.

Bridge

I am cho - sen, not for - sak - en. I

am who You say I am. You are for me, not a -

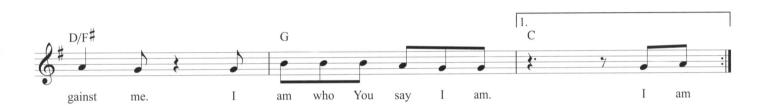

gainst me. I am who You say I am. I am

D.S. al Coda
(take 2nd ending)

I am who You say I am._____ Who the

⊕ **Coda**

Outro

In my Fa - ther's home there's a place for

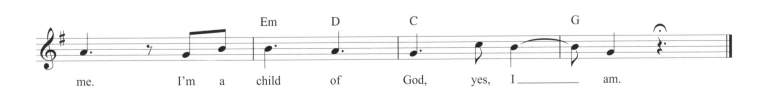

me. I'm a child of God, yes, I_____ am.

You Are My King
(Amazing Love)

Words and Music by Billy James Foote

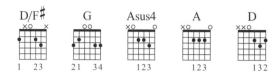

Verse
Moderately, in 2

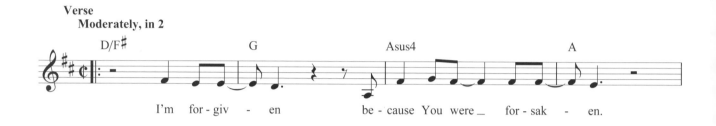

I'm for-giv-en be-cause You were __ for-sak-en.

I'm ac-cept-ed; You were con-demned. __

I'm a-live __ and well; __ Your Spir-it is __ with-in __ me be-

cause You died __ and rose __ a-gain. __

Chorus

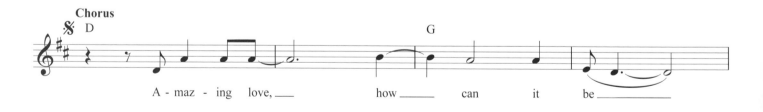

A-maz-ing love, __ how __ can it be __

that You, my __ King, __ would die __ for me? __

A - maz - ing love, ___ I ___ know it's true; ___

it's my ___ joy ___ to hon - or You. ___ In all ___ I ___

___ do, ___ I hon - or You. ___ You ___ are ___ my ___

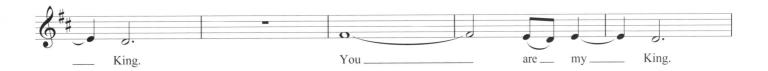

___ King. You ___ are ___ my ___ King.

Je - sus, You ___ are ___ my ___ King. Je - sus,

You ___ are ___ my ___ King.

In all ___ I ___ do, ___ I hon - or You. ___

Your Grace Is Enough

Words and Music by Matt Maher

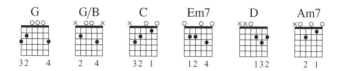

Verse
Moderately fast

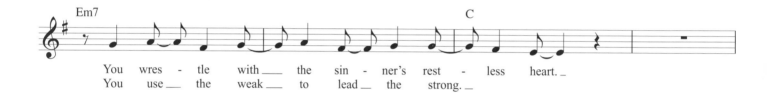

1. Great is ___ Your faith - ful - ness,_ O   God, ___
2. Great is ___ Your love ___ and jus - tice, God ___ of   Ja - cob.

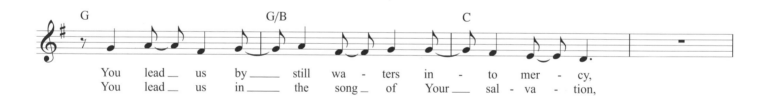

You wres - tle with ___ the sin - ner's rest - less heart. _
You use ___ the weak ___ to lead ___ the strong. _

You lead ___ us   by _____ still wa - ters in - to mer - cy,
You lead ___ us   in _____ the song _ of Your ___ sal - va - tion,

and noth - ing can ___ keep us ___ a - part. ___}
and all ___ Your peo - ple sing _ a - long. ___}

So re -

Pre-Chorus

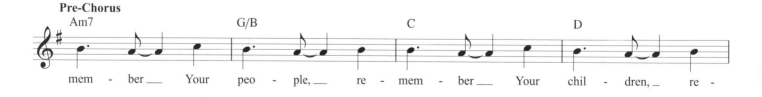

mem - ber ___ Your peo - ple, ___ re - mem - ber ___ Your chil - dren, _ re -

Your Name

Words and Music by Paul Baloche and Glenn Packiam